Unofficial GUIDES JUNIOR

Playing Fortnite: Creative Mode

By Josh Gregory

Metropolitan Library System

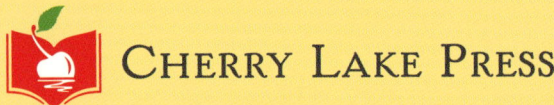

Published in the United States of America by
Cherry Lake Publishing
Ann Arbor, Michigan
www.cherrylakepublishing.com

Reading Adviser: Marla Conn MS, Ed., Literacy specialist, Read-Ability, Inc.

Copyright ©2021 by Cherry Lake Publishing
All rights reserved. No part of this book may be reproduced or utilized in any form or by any means without written permission from the publisher.

Library of Congress Cataloging-in-Publication Data

Names: Gregory, Josh, author.
Title: Playing fortnite : creative mode / by Josh Gregory.
Description: Ann Arbor, Michigan : Cherry Lake Publishing, 2020. | Series: 21st century skills innovation library | Includes bibliographical references and index. | Audience: Grades 2-3 | Summary: "With more than 250 million players around the world, Fortnite is one of the most popular video games in history. In this book, readers will learn how to use the game's powerful Creative Mode, which allows players to build their own Fortnite worlds for others to enjoy. Includes table of contents, author biography, sidebars, glossary, index, and informative backmatter"— Provided by publisher.
Identifiers: LCCN 2020010178 | ISBN 9781534169647 (library binding) | ISBN 9781534171329 (paperback) | ISBN 9781534173163 (pdf) | ISBN 9781534175006 (ebook)
Subjects: LCSH: Fortnite Battle Royale (Game)—Juvenile literature.
Classification: LCC GV1469.35.F67 G7494 2020 | DDC 794.8—dc23
LC record available at https://lccn.loc.gov/2020010178

Cherry Lake Publishing would like to acknowledge the work of the Partnership for 21st Century Learning, a Network of Battelle for Kids. Please visit *http://www.battelleforkids.org/networks/p21* for more information.

Printed in the United States of America
Corporate Graphics

Table of Contents

Play Your Way 5

Getting Started 7

Your Own Island 9

Sky's the Limit 11

Building Up 13

A Special Kind of Smartphone 15

Ready to Go 17

Going Through Galleries 19

Your World, Your Rules 21

Glossary 22

Find Out More 23

Index 24

About the Author 24

All you need is a cool idea to get started with *Fortnite* Creative mode.

Play Your Way

Have you ever had an idea for a new video game? *Fortnite* Creative **mode** can help you make your ideas into reality. You can build whole new worlds for you and your friends to explore. You can also create new game modes that are unlike anything in a regular *Fortnite* match. The possibilities are almost endless!

BATTLE ROYALE

CREATIVE
YOUR ISLANDS. YOUR FRIENDS. YOUR RULES.

PLAY

Like Battle Royale, Creative mode is completely free for anyone who wants to play.

Getting Started

One of the best parts of *Fortnite* Creative mode is that it's very easy to get started. Do you have *Fortnite* installed on your computer, game system, or mobile device? If so, you already have Creative mode. All you need to do is start up *Fortnite* and choose this mode. If you don't have *Fortnite* yet, all you need to do is download it. It's completely free!

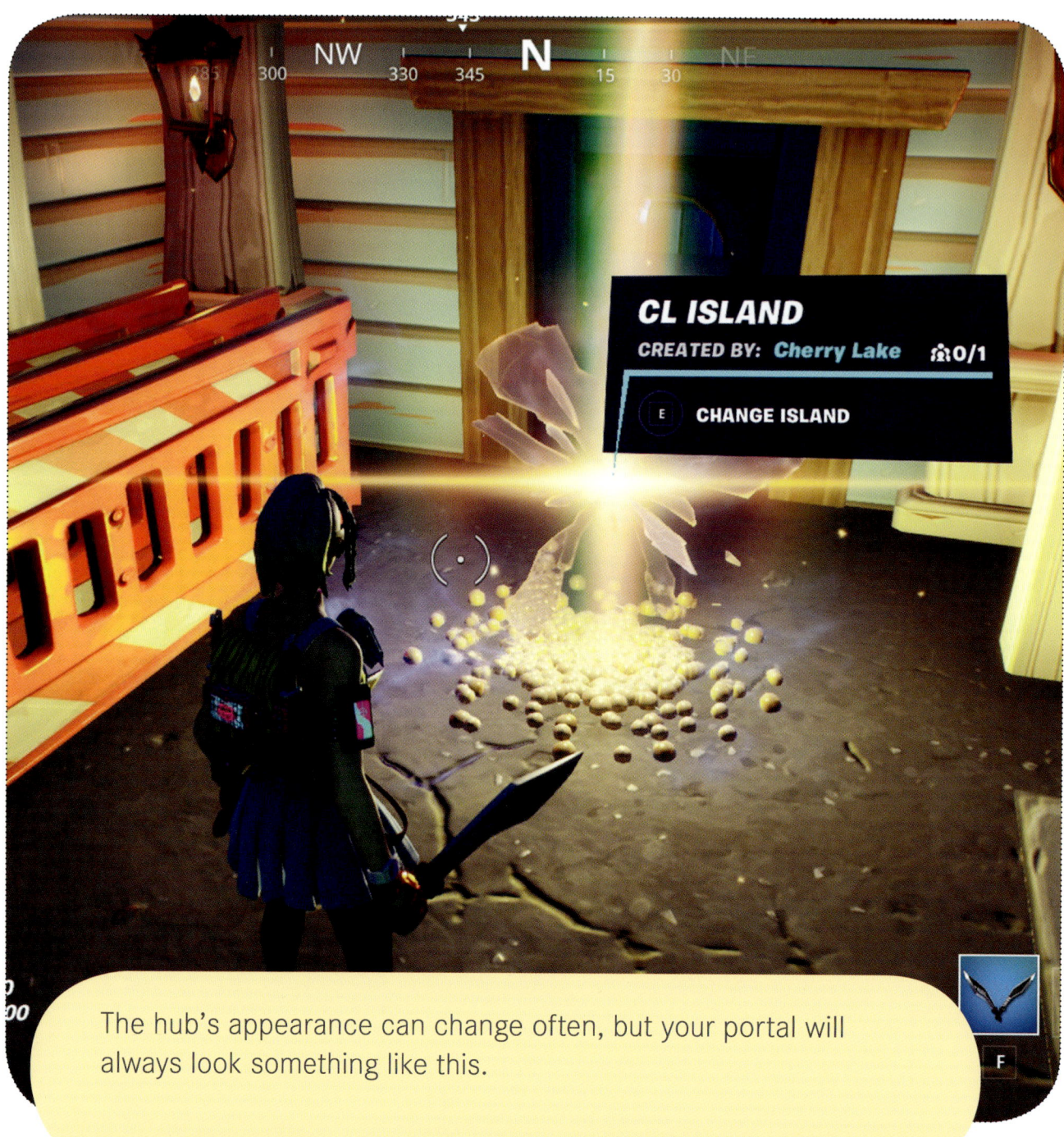

The hub's appearance can change often, but your portal will always look something like this.

Your Own Island

When you start in Creative mode, you will be in an area called the hub. Ahead of you is a glowing **portal**. Run straight into it. You will find yourself dropping down onto an island. This island is your own space where you can build anything you want!

Checking Out the Competition

You don't have to create your own levels to enjoy Creative mode. Choose "Play!" when starting in Creative mode. You will be able to check out the cool things other players have made.

Flying is a great way to get a bird's-eye view of your Creative mode project.

Sky's the Limit

Take a look around your island. It is mostly empty at first. If you want a better view, try flying. Simply press the jump button twice. Now you can zoom through the air! You can get from one end of the island to the other very quickly. Flying also comes in handy when you are building. You can float high above the ground and build tall towers.

If you tried to build something like this during a Battle Royale match, you would need a lot of materials. And someone would probably destroy it before you were finished!

Building Up

One way to make things in Creative mode is to build just like you do in a regular *Fortnite* match. You can build walls, floors, ramps, and roofs. You can use wood, stone, or metal to build these shapes. You get unlimited building **materials** in Creative mode. This means you don't need to chop down trees or break rocks before you build.

Making Memories

In Creative mode there is a meter at the top of the screen. It is labeled "Memory Used." The more you build, the more the meter fills. If it fills up all the way, you can't build more until you delete something.

When an object is highlighted like this, you can use your smartphone on it.

A Special Kind of Smartphone

Another special feature in Creative mode is the smartphone. This tool helps make building faster and easier. Take it out and aim it at a tree or some other object. The object will turn blue. Now look at the left side of the screen. You will see a list of options. For example, you can make a copy of an object, delete it, or rotate it. Play around and see what you can do with the smartphone!

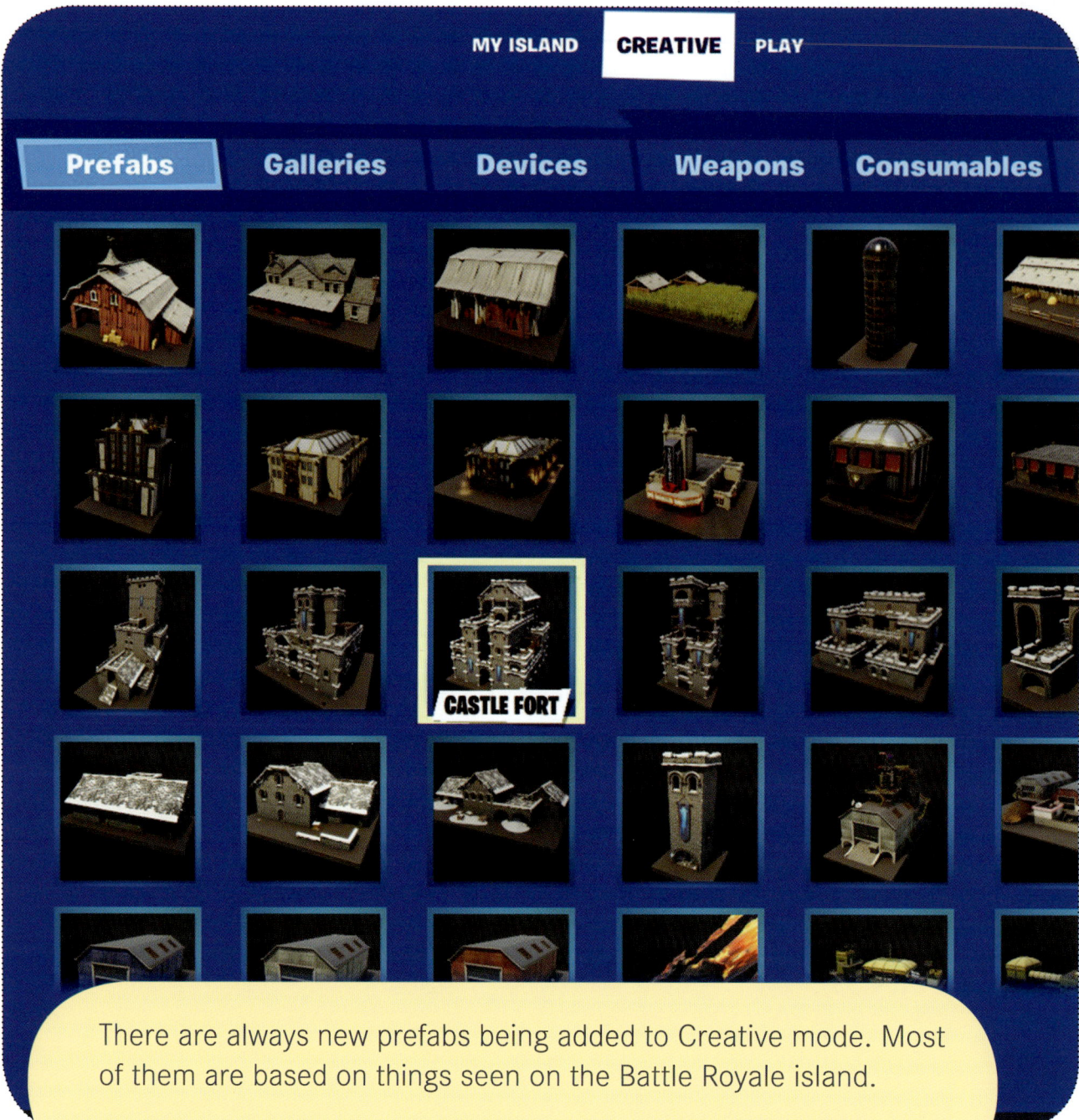

There are always new prefabs being added to Creative mode. Most of them are based on things seen on the Battle Royale island.

Ready to Go

You can also build faster using **prefabs**. Open your **inventory** screen. Then select the "Prefabs" tab. You should see everything from castles to log cabins. You can place any of these buildings on your island. They will be fully built. You can add onto them if you like. You can also use your smartphone to remove or copy pieces of a prefab.

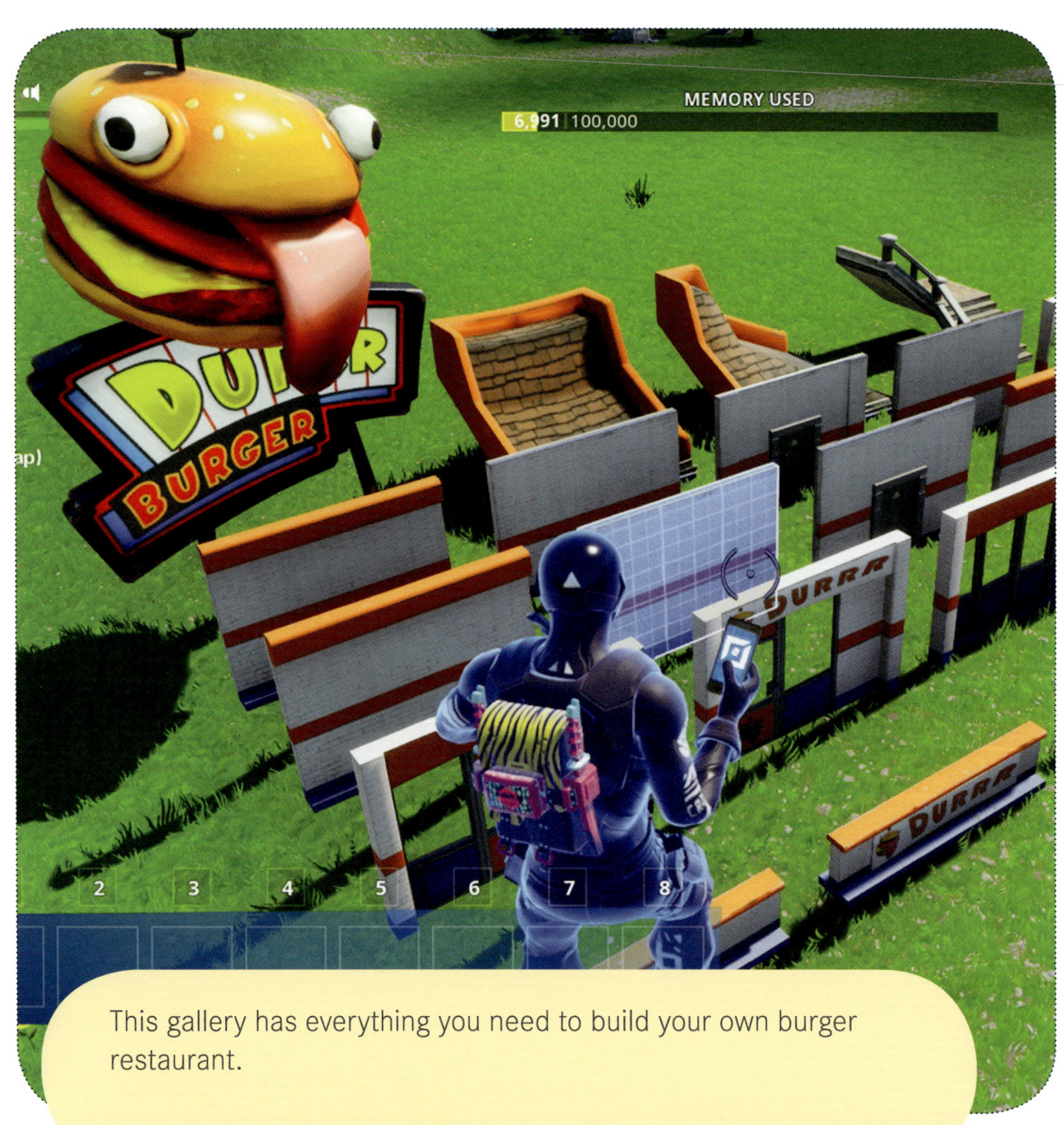

This gallery has everything you need to build your own burger restaurant.

Going Through Galleries

Your inventory screen also has a tab labeled "Galleries." Select it and you will see different groups of themed objects. For example, there are galleries that contain lots of different trees. Others have cars, street signs, and other cool objects. Drop a gallery onto your island. Then use your smartphone to copy and move the different parts you want to use.

UI	**TOOLS**	**DESCRIPTION**	**PERMISSIONS**
RESPAWN TIME			5 SECONDS
SPAWN IMMUNITY TIME			DEFAULT
FALL DAMAGE			OFF
GRAVITY			NORMAL
JUMP FATIGUE			ON
GLIDER REDEPLOY			ON
PLAYER FLIGHT			◀ OFF
PLAYER FLIGHT SPRINT			ON
FLIGHT SPEED			1.0X
PLAYER NAMES & LOCATION			TEAM ONLY

Tabs: **MY ISLAND** / CREATIVE / PLAY

Determines whether players are able to fly during the game.

Want to let other players fly while playing on your island? Simply set "Player Flight" to "on" in the "My Island" menu.

Your World, Your Rules

You can even change all kinds of game rules on your island. Open the inventory and go to the "My Island" tab. There are dozens of settings you can change. Play around with the options and see what you like best. Experimenting is half the fun in Creative mode!

The Next Steps

Do you enjoy building in Creative mode? You might have what it takes to be a pro game **developer**. Keep practicing and learning new things. One day, you might create a game as popular as *Fortnite*!

Glossary

developer (dih-VEL-uh-pur) someone who makes video games or other computer programs

inventory (IN-vuhn-toh-ree) a list of the items your character is carrying

materials (muh-TEER-ee-uhls) supplies needed to build something

mode (MOHD) a way of playing *Fortnite*, with a unique set of rules and goals

portal (PORE-tuhl) an entrance that leads from one place to another

prefabs (PREE-fabs) pre-built structures you can add to your Creative mode island

Find Out More

Books
Cunningham, Kevin. *Video Game Designer*. Ann Arbor, MI: Cherry Lake Publishing, 2016.

Powell, Marie. *Asking Questions About Video Games*. Ann Arbor, MI: Cherry Lake Publishing, 2016.

Web Sites
Epic Games—Fortnite
www.epicgames.com/fortnite/en-US/home
Check out the official *Fortnite* website.

Fortnite Wiki
https://fortnite.gamepedia.com/Fortnite_Wiki
This fan-made website offers up-to-date information on the latest additions to *Fortnite*.

Index

building materials, 13
buildings, 17

copying, 15, 17, 19

developers, 21
download, 7

flying, 11

galleries, 19

hub, 9

installation, 7
inventory, 17, 19, 21
island, 9, 11, 21

memory meter, 13

"Play!" option, 9
portal, 9
prefabs, 17

rules, 21

smartphone, 15, 17, 19

About the Author

Josh Gregory is the author of more than 150 books for kids. He has written about everything from animals to technology to history. A graduate of the University of Missouri–Columbia, he currently lives in Chicago, Illinois.

DISCARD/SOLD
FRIENDS MLS